DANCING WORDS

Dancing Words

A Poetry Collection

JOCELYNE SMALLIAN-KHAN

Smallian-Khan Ltd.

Contents

Dedication vii

Carnivale 1

The Dancer 2

A Dance 3

Tannoura 4

Tannoura Tannoura Tannoura 5

Zeffah 6

Can Can 7

À La Barre 8

Dancacrostic 10

You Are The Dance 11

Carried Away 12

Dabke 13

Ghaziya 14

Ghawazi	15
ArtWorkEthic	16
Two Haiku For Zahra	17
Musician And Dancer	18
Nritya	19
Nuance	20
Made It Right	21
Dancing For Me	22
The Heart Still Dances	23
She Danced	24
Temple Dancer	26
En Pointe	27
Tease	28
Rhumba	29
Art Beat	30
Snazzy Jazzy	31
Express The Dance	32
In The Studio	33
About The Author	34
Also from Jocelyne Smallian-Khan	35

Dedication

To my dance
teachers, mentors,
colleagues, peers,
students, and friends

You are legion
You are vital

You empower
You inspire

Please
never stop being
who you are.

Copyright © 2022 by Jocelyne Smallian-Khan

All rights reserved. No part of this book may be reproduced in any manner whatsoever without written permission except in the case of brief quotations embodied in critical articles and reviews.

First Printing, 2022

For information contact:
   jjsmalliankhan@gmail.com
   http://www.jjsk.ca

Carnivale

For Bernie

Winding - shining - sparkling - free

Festive - blissful - dance with me

The Dancer

For Johanne

The waist
      The hips
The ankle
      The wrist

The eyes
      The fingers
The shoulder
      The leg

The body
      The essence
The spirit
      The soul.

A Dance

For Pam

A pose
      A smile
            A gesture
                   A look
A turn
      A stance
            A step
                  A glance
An expression
            An inflection
                      An exchange
                              A connection
A movement
          A motion
                A maneuver
                        A moment
An intention
          A shift
              An offering
                    A gift

Tannoura

For Cathy

Tannoura, Tannoura,
Twirling entertainment
Tannoura

Tannoura, Tannoura,
Spinning festive colour
Tannoura

Tannoura, Tannoura,
Circling skirt flying high
Tannoura

Tannoura, Tannoura,
Round and round in a trance
Tannoura

Tannoura, Tannoura,
Whirling devotion dance
Tannoura.

Tannoura
Tannoura
Tannoura

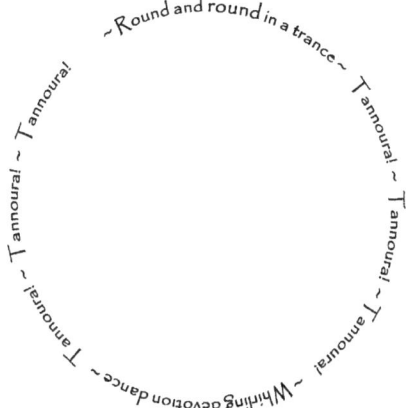

~ Round and round in a trance ~ Tannoura! ~ Tannoura! ~ Tannoura! ~ Whirling devotion dance ~ Tannoura! ~ Tannoura!

Zeffah

For Denise

A single zagharuta calls out
Friends and family rejoice
The rhythm begins

Doum tek tek tek tek doum tek tek

Sagat ringing sounds of elation
Shamadan sparkles in celebration
Candles ablaze

Doum tek tek tek tek doum tek tek

The procession advances
To a chorus of zaghareet
Parade of happiness

Doum tek tek tek tek doum tek tek

The party moves forward
Almeh leads the couple
Their first steps in the world as one.

Can Can

For Ginette

Impromptu
Up on a chair
Pure celebration
For us and for you

Sweet abandon
Innocent freedom
Embodiment of joy
A lesson for the ages.

À La Barre

For Elaine

Battement devant
Battement côté
Battement derrière
Battement côté

Demi-plié
Relevé
Demi-pointe
Détourné

Répète, répète
Répète, répète
Répète, répète
Répète, répète

Battement devant
Battement côté
Battement derrière
Battement côté

Demi-plié
Relevé
Demi-pointe
Détourné

Répète encore
Répète encore
Répète encore
Répète encore

Battement devant
Battement côté
Battement derrière
Battement côté

Demi-plié
Relevé
Demi-pointe
Détourné

Répète, répète
Répète, répète
Répète, répète
Répète, répète

Encore, encore
Encore, encore
Encore, encore
Encore, encore

Dancacrostic

For Hadia

Deploying the body
As ethereal implement
Negotiating the space
Creating experience
Express what words can't convey.

You Are the Dance

For Aziza

You exist
One with movement
Undulate, sway and turn

Abandon limits
Revel in motion
Express the music

Twirl, step and jump
Have no hesitation
Enchant your audience

Dance for eternity
Articulation of spirit
Nuanced expression
Creative somatic
Enduring identity.

Carried Away

For Gwen

Carried away on a tune
Floating away on the air

Tripping on a cloud of sound
Swept away by the breeze

Soaring on sound waves
Vibrating in the wind

Swirling on sound waves
Trembling with the beat

Music carries you away
Acoustic made visual.

Dabke

For Zeinab and Elias

Hand in hand
    Shoulder to shoulder
        Winding line
           Stepping and stomping
              in celebration
              in strength
              in solidarity
        Rhythmic movement
           in unison
Generations gathered
           Pride of a people.

Ghaziya

For Khariya

Khariya dances
Her ancestors in her hips
Audience conquered

Invading their hearts
Celebration of culture
The last of a line.

Ghawazi

For Jalilah

Brass domes on fingers
Singing, ringing, bringing joy
Dancing Ghawazi.

ArtWorkEthic

For Lisa-Marie

Heart races
      This is art
Sweat drips
      This is work.

Two Haiku for Zahra

For Rosemary

In the Wings

The drum beat played on
Doum tekka tekka doum
The dancer waited

Doumbek and Dancer

The doumbek calls out
Doum tekka doum tekka doum
The dancer responds.

Musician and Dancer

For Karim

Musician and dancer
One and the same
Artist with intention
Celebrating culture

Activating the body
Shaping the mind
Influencing the spirit
Inspiring the soul

Singular persistence
Multitudes of impact
Defying ignorance
Dispersing tolerance

Art is political
Creative resistance
Poetic perseverance
Sound and movement activism.

Nritya

For Amrita

Ancient rhythms
Feet slapping
Heartbeat tempo
Pure grace

Carried away
Ecstatic joy
Meditative movement
Expressive emotion

Dance is worship
Dance is healing
Dance is union
Dance is life.

Nuance

For Anne-Marie

Sweep of the eyes
Speaking volumes with a glance

Trace of the fingertips
Reciting legends with a gesture

Catch of the breath
Commanding attention with air

Dwell of the pause
Proclaiming truths with stillness.

Made It Right

For Helena

I couldn't dance anymore.
I'd lost the lively feeling.
The rhythm didn't move me.
No movement was appealing.

My mood was stillness,
not motion.
My ear heard silence,
not music.

But then I danced anyway
And everything was right again.

Dancing For Me

For Vera

Today I danced
      for no one
           but myself.

Perhaps my most
      important
           audience.

The Heart Still Dances

For Laura

The knees ache
    The hips are stiff
        Stride no longer spry
            Legs no longer limber
                But the heart still dances on.

She Danced

For Joan

She told me once that
The closer she got to leaving him,
The redder her hair got

And through all of that.
She danced.

She persevered
Along the ups and downs
Of life's challenges,

And through all of that,
She danced.

She raised her sons,
Creative and considerate men
Breaking a chain of pain.

And through all of that.
She danced

She guided her students,
Helped them grow and flourish,
Supported their dreams.

And through all of that,
She danced.

Their wishes before hers,
Meeting everyone's needs,
Giving of herself always.

And through all of that,
She danced.

Temple Dancer

Temple Dancer carved in stone
Posed here for a thousand years
Do your legs ever get tired?

En Pointe

The pink satin slipper
Shrouds a foot warped

The shiny sheath
Embraces toes gnarled

Delicate elegance
Conceals bones deformed

Pretty covers ugly
Playful veils toil.

Tease

Flirting feather fans
      cleverly conceal
An ankle, a shoulder
      coquettishly revealed
A wink and smile
      teasing with zeal
Flash growing bolder
      the art of the peel.

Rhumba

Slow-quick-quick
      Forward and back
Slow-quick-quick
      Lean and trip
Slow-quick-quick
      Fall and catch
Slow-quick-quick
      Swinging hips

Slow-quick-quick
      Slide and glide
Slow-quick-quick
      Tilt and charm
Slow-quick-quick
      Side to side
Slow-quick-quick
      Arm in arm

Art Beat

Bebop don't stop
Hip hop mic drop

Leave my seat
Drop a beat
Beat the heat
Treat my feet

Bebop don't stop
Hip hop mic drop

Slick as art
Stop and start
Play the part
Break my heart

Bebop don't stop
Hip hop mic drop.

Snazzy Jazzy

Snazzy jazzy
Fizzy fazzy
Whirly swirly
Slumpy surley

Razzle dazzle
Snizzle snazzle
Twizzle fizzle
Swizzle spizzle

Turning churning
Yawning yearning
Slippy trippy
Frumpy frippy

Swish, slam, bam,
Now that was a jam!

Express The Dance

With a leap and a pose,
A story was told.

A gesture and stance,
Expressing the dance.

In The Studio

For all my dance friends

Outside of these walls,
We are many things

Mothers and sisters,
Doctors and clerks.

Neighbours and caregivers,
Daughters and wives.

Accountants and analysts,
Students and teachers.

Inside these walls,
Outside world shed;

Transformed here,
We are dancers.

Jocelyne Smallian-Khan is reigniting a passion for creative writing after many years of being focussed on works of mundanity such as briefing notes, audit reports, and business plans. In addition to her government job, reading books, drinking tea, riding motorcycles, travelling, and scribbling poems, she is a dance teacher, the owner of Duniya Dance Studio (www.DuniyaStudio.com), and also used to perform Egyptian dance (Raqs Baladi and Raqs Sharqi) for several years.

Her poems have also appeared in *It Sounded Like Darkness: a poetry collection* and *Rain Dropped Softly: A Poetry Collection* (both available on Amazon) edited by David Allan Hamilton, and in *Pocket Lint,* a little lit magazine by Warren Dean Fulton / Gnurr Productions Inc.

Dancing Words is her second chapbook, containing short bits dedicated to dance-related subjects. Her first chapbook of poetry, *The Muted Muse*, a lighthearted exploration of writer's block, was published in January 2022.

Visit her website for more information and random scribbles: www.jjsk.ca.

Also from Jocelyne Smallian-Khan

The Muted Muse: A Poetry Collection (January 2022)

Friends and Family: A Poetry Collection (forthcoming)

Barren Ground: A Poetry Collection (forthcoming)

Taking Flight: A Poetry Collection (forthcoming)

Instersectscars: A Poetry Collection (forthcoming)

www.ingramcontent.com/pod-product-compliance
Lightning Source LLC
Chambersburg PA
CBHW050209130526
44590CB00043B/3362